Sage's writings provide an exceptionally wide range of inspiration that offers something for everyone.

Shad Diamond, Ph.D

Sage Walker has written a powerfully compelling book guiding the reader into the sacred mysteries of loss, sorrow, love, and healing. On the path to our highest source, she shares perspectives for increasing self-awareness and joy in your life.

Reading these messages, you peel the layers off and expand your heart each time you read a passage. These are critically important at this time as we all need to be the best person we can be.

Lynn Schramel
Teacher

To Lisa –   April 28, 2023

Have a great day
every day!

Peg ♥
♀♀

The
Awakening

CREATING A NEW WAY OF BEING

SAGE WALKER

Paperback ISBN: 978-1-64184-238-9
Ebook ISBN: 978-1-64184-239-6

Acknowledgments

Along this journey, many people have assisted me, and for all who helped, I am very grateful. To the people who showed up in my life so I could obtain the information and to the realm of Spirit who guide me in this work, I am grateful. I thank my friends including Lynn Schrammel, Johanna Woodside, Sue Cook, Shad Diamond, Joe Roscoe, Denise Lensenski, Barbara Campbell, Pam Perkins, and all members of the Healing Light Group for their encouragement and support.

There are many others who have supported and encouraged me to bring this into a reality. For all the help I received from anyone I am grateful as it kept me moving forward to publication. Great thanks to my publisher, Sharon CassanoLochman, for supporting and assisting me in this venture. It has been a new and sometimes daunting journey.

I am also very grateful for the gift of being able to do this work to help others on their path out of their darkness and into a better life. This is a true blessing and my hope is these words can assist many others to enjoy a better life. My wish is that all who read these words, their life is changed for the better.

Authors Note

Many times, we will meet obstacles that seem much bigger than they are. Sometimes it is because we have no faith in ourselves, and our world has become small and limited. These limits we put there. They may be as simple as "This is all there is for me," or "I can't have what I want." These beliefs are past judgments that stop us from dreaming or growing.

When our world is so small and restricted, we lose some of our energy to be more, to have dreams, and to enjoy our day-to-day lives. Recently, my world became very limited because I was absorbed in the negativity of a situation in my life. I withdrew and physically became more tired and involved in my struggles. I was unable to cope with the bumps in the road and became immersed in negativity and wondered, "What did I do wrong?"

I did not think others would want to hear my troubles. Also, in fear of being judged, I did not want anyone to see my struggles or to share my pain. It felt so heavy that I could not see beyond the struggle. My world was so closed. Some part of me thought, "What did I do to deserve this?" I moved through my day on autopilot with a false smile on my face.

One day I decided this was not how I wanted to live. When I started to change and come out of my struggle, I went back to my old positive and talkative self, had more energy and reached out to friends. The world put what I needed in my path. I had to do my part and change my limited world.

It may not be easy to move beyond our fears and doubts and to open ourselves and share. Moving beyond our comfort zone sometimes is a struggle, but I'll walk with you as you change also. We can give each other our time and listen to each other's struggles, big and small.

Our inner voice only tells us what you learned and were told as you were growing up. It is a record on continuous play and only stops when you open to the truth. So, examine it and see if it is your truth today.

You change this voice when you see your true selves and become aware of your old and negative beliefs. You can look at them and then throw away those that are no longer truth and fill your souls up with new beliefs. You can change and be free of restrictions and make our world a better place today.

In all the messages he or she is interchangeable.

Introduction

A great way to use this book is to look at a title that appeals to you. After reading it think about it and has this message been a part of your life at any time. Ask yourself if you are holding anything around that experience and then recognize it is ok to let it go as it is your past, not your present.

May you be blessed with awareness and become free of old issues. It is your time to shine and show the world who you are. I hope these help you to learn more about yourself and give you a gift of a happier life.

Blessings

Table of Contents

A Blessing

May the Light of your Soul guide you.
May the light of your soul bless the work you do,
With the secret love and warmth of your heart.
May you see in what you do the beauty of your own soul.
May the sacredness of your work bring healing, light, and renewal.
May it be brought to those who work with you
And to those who see and receive your work.
May your work never weary you.
May it release within you wellsprings of refreshing energy,
Inspiration, and excitement.
May you be present in what you do.
May you never become lost in the bland absences of life.
May the day never burden you.
May dawn find you awake and alert,
Approaching your new day with dreams,
Possibilities and promises.
May evening find you gracious and fulfilled.
May you go into the night blessed, sheltered and protected.
May your soul calm, console and renew you

A Guide

I come alone.
I go the same way.
I give you guidance,
Upon this day.
Touch my spirit.
Touch my soul.
It is the light,
You will know.
The work that comes,
Will be to move a stone.
You know this stone or lesson,
Is your own.
Spirit will guide so you may see,
The future for me and thee.
Trace this path for it will run
As it flows, too and from.
Know yourself (your spirit)
And live in peace,
Within and without, for it is the grease.
You more than others need to know,
How YOU reap and sow.
A part of you wars inside and stops you,
Much more than you know.
Let your spirit guide you,
To a safer place, inside of you,
Where you can feel internally safe.
A spot, a place, that dark little hole inside,
Will fade, as you will know you are safe.
Listen to the guides, let them know you understand,
The powerful place in this world you hold.
It is sacred, it is real,
And for you a new deal.
Uncover it. Uncover it.
Bless it too, for it's the truth.
Hiding inside of you.

A Soul

A soul locked up,
Yearning to be free.
Not knowing it's worth,
To you and me.
Living in fear,
Of being the real person,
Afraid of all that life may bring.
Not knowing the gentleness and strength,
Emanating from within,
That all others see.
Life's a journey for you and me,
Giving us lessons and blessings.
When we care we see all the soul can be,
Giving to others who need to be free.
The soul pokes out yearning to be free,
Because it can't be kept down, you see.
It is a precious giver of gifts,
Which this soul does not yet know.
Some are for her and some are for him.
And then some are for me and you.

A Place I Was at In Life

It's not a place,
I wanted to be.
It has been a home,
To all my memories.
Sometimes it felt good.
Sometimes it felt bad.
Fear, anger, sadness,
Love, joy, and visions of grandness.
Sometimes I lived here.
Sometimes I hid here.
It was a space,
I was connected to.
Here I faced fears, took giant steps,
And little ones too on this pathway of life.
I faced lost love and felt sadness too.
I faced spiritual growth and felt its joy.
It now holds me with all these things.
It says I'm home I'm going to be all I can be.
Now it's time to move on.
Time to change.
Time for more growth
And new adventures,
To put in my mental picture frames.
It's served a purpose in my life.
I release and I let it go,
As I enter my new life's picture show.
The next step goes up on the ladder of life.
I enter this new place,
Where I will find joy and peace,
For myself and all mankind.
New adventures.
New journeys.
Happier ones too,
Leads me to the next phase,
Of my life's journey.

A Long Way

A long walk it has been.
Through muddy waters and great storms.
Lonely, scared, defiant and lost, was this little girl.
Unsure of what to do, how to act, where to go.
Searching, looking, hoping, seeking.
Torn and tattered, the lost angel was seeking.
She knew not who she was.
She could not see she was blessed,
With an angel inside,
Trying to look out.
It's beauty so rare and beyond compare.
It's just waiting for its turn to share.
Who is this angel?
She did not know, for she could not see her gifts,
Those you and I know.
It's you, the one inside, the you that you still hide.
She loves, she cares for all her friends,
But for herself, she does not dare.
She gives us gifts of who she is
And shares her wisdom too,
As that's one of her gifts.
She helps all she can and never complains.
She does not see her own needs as she helps all she can.
Save a little for yourself, for you deserve that and more.
Life is a precious gift that you give.
You are a great spirit who gives of herself.

As I walk through life, I have watched many men and women who this
is about. They do not often see their blessings. They are also unaware of
the true gift they are to the world.

Angel Words

Angel words come to all who love.
Listen to the whisper.
Listen to the voice.
They bring hope and change,
On the winds of time,
Coming to you and mine.
Bless this world.
Pray for peace.
Do your part,
Love your neighbor,
And the crazy person next door.
Know they live locked in an unknown world.
Bless them each day.
Hope that they may pray to be released,
From their discomfort each passing day.
We all have a part,
We need to play.
Live. Love. Pray.
Do this for you and your neighbors each day.

Thanks

Believe

We bring you peace, love, and joy.
Look at it as a toy
With which to play,
During some part of your day.
We come in your time of need,
So it may become a seed.
A small ball this toy is
For you to make large,
For as long as you live.
Find ways to make it bigger,
See it grow and expand.
Now life will no longer be angry or bland.
There are many here
That you don't see.
Believe. Believe. Believe.

Friends Blessings

People whose worth is beyond measure.
People too value and treasure.
Friends ask for nothing but are quietly there
during stress and emotional turmoil.
Kindness, comfort and nurturing comes in many forms.
It is sometimes difficult to receive and teaches us to bend
And not be rigid in our pain.
Acceptance of the gift of friends is a way to honor them and to grow.
They give to us again and again; on that, we can depend.
They are the blessings in our lives which I hope never ends.
My prayer is that we all have friends in our lives.
Bless all of them.
Hopefully, in their lives, there are many friends.
I ask that the blessings they give, to them it returns tenfold.

Ancestors Call

Ancestors call you to the bridge.
Ancestors call that you may know.
Ancestors call that it comes from within.
Ancestors call you to the bridge to inner peace
And inner peace of mind.
Ancestors call because you are supposed to be here.
Ancestors call that you may give a blessing to all.
Ancestors call that you may listen.
Ancestors call that you may hear.
Ancestors call that you know we are here.
Ancestors call so pleased that you may know them.
Ancestors call to you as you go to the inner peace that flows.
Ancestors call to the love of life, God and You

I Am There

If I came and you never saw me.
If I helped and you didn't notice.
If I am walking with you and you do not notice.
If you felt alone and I was right beside you.
This is what happens, each day, every moment.
This is why I cry because you do not see me.
Allow me to be with you.
Know when you ask, I am there.
Know when you hurt, I am beside you.
Know in all life's challenges, great and small,
I am there.
Reach for me even in small ways,
Such as opening your hand so I may hold it.
Just think of me and am I am there.
Just allow me to be with you always.

It's Time to Look at You Now

We are at a critical time for each of us.
Time to review who we are.
Time to stop hiding any aspect of ourselves.
Time to embrace the parts we like
And the parts we are not proud of.
It is all of us, which is perfect as is.
One cannot exist without the other.
They both help us grow and change.
It is the parts we don't like which nudge us to make changes.
It is the part we like that shows us how to live fully.
So, embrace all of you.
You are perfect, wise and complete.
So, listen to your inner wisdom.
You were created like this to create a better life
And to be a guide to others.
So, don't hold back. Just *be*.
Allow the world to see all of you.
It truly needs you present now.

Transformation

Listen to the message.
Forget the pain.
Now and forever it will never be the same.
Look for the pain and pull it out.
Look and pull for yourself to become new.
Fill. Fill the garden of your soul,
For it will take you far.
Build the flowers (good feelings).
Feed your soul and allow light in.
This brings far more than you will know.
Let this come in and fill you inside your skin.
Pull all the good in. Pull. Pull.
Allow the light to fill your soul.
Allow the light to heal your soul.
Allow the light to fill the spaces within.
Be what you want you to be.
Fill your soul and set it free.
It is your anchor.
Fill your soul with the knowledge of the real you
And it will be anchored now and evermore.
Let peace begin.
Let peace be a part of your renewed soul.

Family

Family-A group of people who are supposed to love you.
Family-A group of people who often don't know you.
Family-A group of people who choose to see you as they believe you are.
Family-A choice we can't make and a choice we can make.
Feelings of family-A warm safe, serene and loving feeling.
Feelings of family are families we chose.
Those who are our true family

Wandering

Through wandering ways.
We get where we belong.
Some of the time full of Sorrow,
But then again, we are full of song.
Some of our songs we sing inside,
Others we sing to those on the outside.
Our songs are the best of ourselves.
Those things we don't always see,
Sometimes we get help from human elves to see them.
They help us know the soul of us,
That we may show the world our light.
This is our path and that is our purpose to see that light.
Ours, others and that of all souls,
To see that spot inside that always shines,
That God and others may know.

Memories

The fabric of our lives.
The things we keep.
The things we wish,
We could throw away.
Most are pleasant,
Beautiful, nurturing and calming.
They structure our living.
Remember a scene.
A favorite place.
A favorite person.
Remember your dreams,
Your goals, your aspirations.
They are the memories
For your future to gleam.
All these things spin inside,
Where our soul resides.
Blend, weave, strengthen and then shore them up.
All things here and in the future galore.
Never give up,
Only weed them out.
Use the best ones,
So your strength can stand out.

Life Changes

They come at the time we need them.
They are always to grow.
They allow you to expand,
And create a new you.
They are sometimes hard but sometimes easy.
Follow the joy and the light of the new.
Forget the doubt,
Leave the fear behind.
Know these are traps and impede your progress.
Touch into new adventures.
It is a time to expand,
To be joyful and to leave behind stagnant energy.
Take your love of life,
Your joy, your creativity,
Into all you do.
Bring the love of your family,
Into a new place.
Be alive. Be free.
Know and trust yourself.

Ashlee

Death to us,
Much sorrow it brings.
To those who pass,
It brings Angel Wings.
Our sorrow so hard,
It's often overwhelming to bear.
To them, it's freedom to fly in the sky,
Without Fear.
They do all things, they run, and they play.
As they live in all the joy it brings.
Ashlee will fly as others do.
She'll help others from her place in the sky.
A star will get a new name for it is hers
And now will never be the same.
Written for Ashlee Tellier as she passed away

Gentle Power

Loving caring,
Nurturing and balanced too.
What lives within, lives without too.
Mother, daughter, sister, friend.
She moves, weaves and blends.
Unobtrusive, quiet but full of power too.
She knows not her power, but that's her glue.
Learned and lived in from life's school.
She's honest, creative and solid within,
For she is never a fool.
Life's choices make her who she is.
Centered in her space,
Living in her bliss (peace and passion).

A Lady

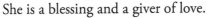

An angel who assists others as they travel life's journey,
With its many twists and turns.
One who quietly does what she can in a gentle and peaceful way.
She knows life and its twists and turns.
She gives us freedom and encourages us to be all we can be.
She is a Blessing for many who have traveled,
The journey with her, quietly with love.
She is an angel in others' lives.
She is a blessing and a giver of love.

A Path

A path you go down,
Learning lessons,
And sometimes living with a frown.
Closed and full of fear,
Looking but never seeing the sun.
These things you and I experienced,
In each and every way,
Are a part of our growth.
Lessons to show where you've been.
Lessons to show where you need to go.
Each step you take, you make a choice.
Good, bad, backward or forward,
Only to learn another lesson with a smack.
On and on to see the beauty of you and me,
Stripping the junk which covers the real you and me.
Little were you seeing the beautiful person,
Who was hiding behind the pain?
No smiling or seeing the person you and I had become.
Lifting this veil, you and I now can see the difference between
Them and me.
When I stretch out of the pain and struggle,
The world responds and presents what I need.

A Star Who Shines

A star who shines,
Sometimes a light so dim,
It is hard to see a beacon hide's within.
Kindness and compassion in her soul,
Ever needing love before she feels old.
The beacon waits to be turned on,
To shine for all to see.
It hides behind guilt, fear, and shame.
Be Who You Really Are.

Be Who You Are

Be who you are,
Because it is this person the world needs now.
Believe. Believe.
Trust that we know you.
Trust that we guide you in all your actions.
We walk each step with you.
We hold grace for you always.
Reach for us when confused,
Angry, sad or depressed.
As you do this it shifts you.
Into a higher vibration.
Just a thought changes your world,
As it changes you.
Ask for your greater good,
Gives thanks and allow it to come to you.
You deserve this and even more than you can believe.

Angels Above Watching

Angels above
Watch their angel's below.
This is what you must always know.
Be the giver of love.
Be the receiver of all,
That is so you will not fall.
Believe in angels for you are one.
Live your life,
But don't forget to have some fun.
You have a path,
That's not in your vision.
On this journey, there are some lessons
And these we must walk through.
Live angel.
Find peace so them you may know
And to you, allow their love to flow.

Creating

What are you creating?
How are you creating?
With intent?
With wisdom?
Do you just create randomly?
Time is now for moving,
Into firmly and attentively creating.
Our world needs this.
It also needs examples of responsively creating.
As you create you send love into your creation.
As you do this love comes back to you.
As it flows it encompasses all of you and your aura.
You become a light shining into the world,
These become light beams,
Attracting a loving and peaceful new vibration,
To help your world and all who live within.

Spa Time

As I think of you, I see a beautiful soul.
One not seen by you quite yet.
You are a treasure each moment of your day
And watched from afar.
We ask you to search within,
Your beautiful soul to see what we see.
It's not about being perfect, energetic or creative.
It's about being who you are with the challenges of life.
Just be with the moment and know you as I know you.
You will then see the goodness and beauty of yourself.
I know your heart and soul and value you greatly.
It is an honor to be your friend.
The Angels ask for you to spend Spa time each day.
This is time set aside to just be and allow them to work on you.
They ask for your patience as they care for you.
Also, let them know what you need as they will be happy to help.
So set in your chair each night and let them come.
You need to do nothing as they are overjoyed to be with you.
They bless you and watch over you.
They are your friends.

I wrote this for a friend but it applies to us all.
Give yourself Spa Time today.

Trees

Tall, thin,
Fat and round.
Sparsely covered,
Or full of leaves.
Routed and strong,
Flowing with the wind.
Graceful as it begins,
Nourished by the sun.
Nurtured by the earth.
Stretching from one
Toward the other.
Home to many birds
Who nest in their limbs.
Many things we could learn
If we followed their pattern.
Learn to be the flow.
Live as if you are the strength of the trunk.
Allow yourself to be nurtured by the sun,
The earth and others on your path.
Learn your lessons,
Allowing the wind to help move difficulty along.
Never give up, always keep moving.
Know your journey is about growing,
Like the tree to all its grace and beauty.

The Lady of Curiosity

Hello.
Do you know we are here for you?
We have never left you.
We wish to let you know
What we see in you.
You are a lady of light.
Know you can be this for others and the children.
We need to tell you that you do not see *who you are.*
You are a blessing, so know this truth.
We ask you to see the light in yourself.
This is the beautiful soul you have.
You are precious.
We wish for you to be in joy more often.
Gracious, Loving.
Creative, Humorous,
Beautiful in all ways.
This is our vision of you.
We are your Angel Guides.
We love you unconditionally.
You are all you need to be.
Never doubt our faith and love for you.

The Way We Grow

Sift and change, move and look.
Constant movement, constant change,
In small ways or large.
It's up to you in all ways.
Sometimes there is help,
Sometimes we do it alone.
Never to fail, only to move on
In whatever way we can.
There's always help in one form or another,
You only have to reach for it.
It's here and it's there.
Just hold out your hand
And we'll always be there,
As will those around you who can assist.

Thank-you.
Shanta'

The Changes in My Life

My life now is different
And filled with joy.
I have many friends
Whom I see and enjoy.
I see the bright brilliant skies,
With white fluffy clouds.
I stand in the moonlight,
Feeling it's a bright light.
There are many things to do
And many places to go.
I see many choices
And hear all the caring voices.
So many thanks to all
Who have touched me in many different ways?
You are the blessings
For which in the beginning,
I could not see.

Terry
Life's Struggles

He lived a life of trials and tribulations
And these were always easy to remember.
He seemed torn and in pain at times,
But still, the good aspects of Terry showed through.
In memory of Terry, I want to leave you with some of the memories,
I choose to remember about him.
I choose to remember a father who loved and was proud of his children.
I choose to remember Terry who always cared for Kami.
I choose to remember Terry who cared for
And always visited his mother.
I choose to remember a Terry who loved and showed off his dog.
I choose to remember Terry who was proud of his skills as a mason.
I choose to remember Terry who was working to get his life on track.
I choose to remember a Terry who was finding the goodness
Of who he really was.
I choose to remember Terry who was like a lot of us sometimes.
And even had the same ring tone on his phone as I did.
I choose to remember a Terry who treasured things from his childhood.
I choose to remember Terry who flies high over mountains and valleys.
I choose to remember a Terry who is now free
And watches over those he loved.

We love you Terry
Fly and be free.

The Loss of a Friend

My heart is sad today,
Because I lost a friend.
He walked a long road and had many struggles,
As he walked this road.
He showed great courage and stamina,
Always saying, *"You gotta do what you gotta do."*
His love of others wherever they were, gained him many friends.
He showed us patience, tolerance, faith, courage,
And great love of family and friends.
He was a simple man who had great depth.
He had the love and respect of many in his life.
Today my heart is sad for the loss of my friend.
He lived.
He loved.
He showed us much.
He was always there for each of us.
He didn't judge what we did or who we are.
He said, *"You gotta do what you gotta do."*
If we failed, he'd help us through,
Giving us support and love in a way only he knew.
We honor our friend as to God he went.

To My Friend Jimmy

Ralph

A husband, father, grandfather, brother, and priest,
In tune with the spiritual realm.
He walked his journey giving to those he loved.
He assisted many in need.
He guided them to where they needed to be in life.
He gave of himself to others.
He loved his family beyond measure.
Difficult he could be at times,
Much like his mother.
Both felt they were older and wiser
And should have their way.
They sometimes were butting heads,
Even as they did their love of each other showed.
Funny it was,
But you always knew the end result was love.
He is blessed and now watches from above
And says *"Be Good"*, *"Live Fully"*
As you are watched from above with love".

The Pain of Grief

The pain of grief,
I know it well.
My child. My soul,
Whose loss hurt beyond belief.
So ill he became,
And such loving tender care
Did I give?
I no longer wanted to live.
My soul. My self,
Felt torn from me.
My guilt became a burden to me.
What didn't I do?
What didn't I know?
So, he may have lived
And continue to grow.
I walked in sadness and pain
A very long time.
My burden. My guilt,
Of what I could have done.
A weight has been taken off
So I might see I could do no more,
For him or me.
It became his time,
For his soul to go.

He had fulfilled his purpose,
That I now know.
I walk my road now,
Totally with grace,
Carefully putting my feet in place.
Young seeds of all kinds, I now sow,
In memory of a child of mine,
Who was well known.
He's with God,
In a better place,
As he lives within his grace.
Someday there I'll come,
When my work here is well done.

Shanta

The Chapel of Transfiguration

(Found at the base of the Teton Mountains)

May the beauty of these peaks soothe our souls.
May we always remember their strength, their majesty
And find ours inside.
May we absorb the beauty,
As it reminds us of ours.
May we raise ourselves to their peaks,
And may we have our consciousness rise as high.
May these solid mountain rocks,
Remind us of our path of love.
May we find all of this within.

I was inspired to write this while setting in the Chapel looking at the
Teton Mountains as they stood in the background during my visit. I
visited there several times as I fell the majestic power of these mountains.
I also felt an Angelic portal at the base of the mountains. The Chapel
truly is a sanctuary for those who enter
and I was blessed to discover this treasure.

The Circle of Angels

We see the beauty that lies within.
We see. We see.
There is no room to hide.
We see. We see.
Look. Look and find yourself.
Ask the ego to go and hide.
Look. Look and find yourself.
Be grateful for who you are.
Be aware and know we see all of you.
Be assured we love you
And all that is inside.
We watch as you walk this journey.
We see the blessing of who you are.
We see what you hide.
We see. We see.
Know that what we see is the truth
And we know the greatness of who you are.
Know we watch you from above.
Know we do this with great love.
Know you can never hide from us.
Know we are always there for you.
Know we are here to guide you.
Blessings and Love.

From
The Circle of Angels.

Strife

Strife comes in our lives
Bringing upsets and pain.
Again and again.
What messages?
What lessons,
Do we need to learn?
Strife comes in and out,
Causing us to doubt. what is this life all about.
Oh creator, God or whoever is listening,
Why?
When will it go away?
What can I do,
To help myself break free of the bonds and chains,
So strife will not return again.
Bring me freedom again,
So I may find Peace
And blessed relief.
It is just around to corner,
Which I cannot see,
Because I'm stuck in the struggle you see.

Loving You

You do not see,
Who you are.
You do not see
Your Greatness.
You do not see
The Loving Gift You are.
Do not let life's experiences
Color who you are.
Life is a journey
Not a race to run.
Life is not a time to be run ragged.
Allow love to fill you.
Find the love of you,
That's inside you.
Be one with the gift of your life.
Be one with our friend (You).
Slow down and allow more love
To be found within you.
Be the peace you want to know.
Be the peace to show others how it flows.
Love you.
We know you are a perfect gift,
Walking through life's lessons.

Life's Journey

Life's journey is not always smooth.
It has many twists and turns.
All leading to the place,
You are supposed to go.
Live fully.
Live with love for all things.
Live so you have peace inside.
Live knowing you are enough.
The spiritual journey,
Is not always easy.
It is the most rewarding,
Of all our journeys.

Be at peace each day.
Be loving in all actions.
Be loving and nurturing to yourself.
Be aware you are not alone.

Moving On

Inspired by Rich

You are not your experiences.
Your experiences are what have made you, you.
You are a gift of light in the world.
Honor you as we honor you.
Create a new you from your experiences.
Do not hold on to them, they do not define you now.
They were a guide to move you through trauma,
Into the being of who you are now.
Love yourself as we love you now,
Not as the person you were at the time.
Be willing to let trauma go,
So, you can be the light you are now.
You are never alone,
We are always with you,
So, create with us, not your past.

Sent from those who stand with you always.

I Detach Myself from Pain

I have lived and seen anger, fear, depression,
Hopelessness, bitterness, and withdrawal from a life worth living.
These have addictive power and easily increase.
Once you start down that road it is very difficult to stop.
Take back your *power*.
Realize you are a powerful force greater than any human experience.
Know you have the choice and strength to walk a different path.
The emotions can feel like it's all you know
And comforting because they are strong and addicting.
They help us to feel strong but they push life away from us.
They are usually what was taught to us by people we did not like.
This gives them or the situations *control* over us.
Choose to move beyond that which has had control.
Be the powerful person you are
And walk forward into the unknown because you can.
Let no one hold you in a place of fear or pain.
They are not the source of power, you are.
Life is sometimes a challenge which we need to move beyond.
Bring freedom into your life
As it is the result of taking control and changing your life.

Life's Trials

Life's trials sometimes seem not to end,
But it's only when we are turning back
And can't see around the bend.
The road seems rough as we find our way,
To the Inner Self of who we really are today.
Some will come to us and some will go,
It's their choice of how to live and grow.
Some will pull on us and say, "It's too hard".
Save me, save me, It's your job.
You know the real truth,
That's their job, their own self,
To win or lose.
It's our freedom,
We are fighting for.
It's the curve on the sharp bend,
Where we need not end.
Pushing on
And through sticky stuff.
It's here we find answers,
And gain strength.
For beyond the bend,
The end is in sight.
It's where we'll no longer
Know fear and fright.
The road smooths out,
Bringing Blessings galore.
So, walk we must,
Through all those opening doors.

Nicole

She creates.
She dreams for many things.
And also, for things to be different.
Sometimes she is lonely and sometimes scared.
If she gets quiet and listens to her inside,
She knows she is ok.
She does good things for others.
She needs to do good things for herself,
As she grows her life will change.
Through many lessons, she will go.
Always she will be okay.
Allowing learning even though
She's often yearning for what's next.
She'll see a lot of things as she's learned much from life.
She is a special person whom others will know as she grows.
Great joy and great pride we have in our Nicole.

A Place to Learn and Grow

You come,
As we built a place,
For you to grow.
You became more whole and aware.
You've changed, you've enjoyed,
This precious time and space.
It has been a Blessing to be with you.
It has been a joy to watch you blossom.
We never knew we would walk this journey with you
And that together, in you, we would create a sacred space.
A place that gives us the freedom to help you embrace new ideas.
We honor your teachers who do our work.
They give us the freedom to teach you, Sacred Ones.
They are open and allow us to be with them.
A new time is coming,
A time to use lessons learned.
A time to release all fear and judgment.
Know we are assisting to create a new world.
You have asked to be in this time and place.
You have asked us to come and we did.
You have asked to know and you now do.
Know you are blessed.
Know all is working in Divine Order.
Be at peace, always
Learning never ends.
Blessings are always there.

Believe in You

Believe in who you are.
Know the internal self.
Learn more about you.
The goodness of your inner self,
Wants to grow.
Look at the soul of who you are.
It is here you find the truth.
It is here you learn so you may grow,
Into your potential all of which you do not know.
It is time for you to expand
As the world needs,
Your light, Your Spark.

Courage

He's walked through life with pain and sorrow.
Wondering, why did this happen to me?
He's seen the pain, felt a lot too
And did not know, what to do.
He's made mistakes and learned from them too.
He searched until he found what he can do.
It's hard to look at what to do.
You become afraid and distrustful too.
Sometimes he looks around the corner,
Hoping it will be an easier walk.
He looks slowly at his parents and his past.
Fearing what he'll find in his past.
He's been told a lot of things.
He's been taught and beaten too,
Into a belief which they had of him.
This hooked like chains upon his soul.
The pain, the fear, the anger, the rage,
The sadness, the loneliness inside for him spell danger.
Just yet he cannot see, all the good, the courage,
The strength and beauty, the inside we see.
He was given a message for most of his life,
Which has made him something he did not want to be.
It has given him a gift of which he's not fully aware,
But its slowly changing as he becomes aware.
It's hard to see beyond what you are taught,
But he looks and hopes its good.
Intelligence, strength, an uncommon man,
Who is willing to live beyond the boundary's others would give.
I am glad for the chance to know,
This gentleman of courage.
He's a loving man that the world needs
And we are proud that him we know.
Walk forward each day of your life.
Learn something, about who you are each day,
And you will eventually see,
The man or women of courage you were meant to be.

Finding a Better Life

Life, it's meant to be lived.
Look inside you for the life to be lived.
Give no blame.
Live no fear.
Feel no shame.
Let no anger near.
Find your spark to live from within,
For within it you will find who you will become.
From this space, life is to be lived,
As you go through hurdles you need to forgive.
Pain is a choice from which you can live free,
Once you know yourself better than me.
Love is a gift which you must give,
Unto yourself so you may live.
Live in this space day by day,
Finding your joy in a glorious way.
This is the place you must start,
So, you no longer feel pulled apart.
It'll bring you freedom,
To be the loving self you need to be.

Angel's Gift

Safe, Loved
And held in our arms,
Child of mine.
Trust us.
Feel us.
Know it is the truth.
Now and Forever,
Angels of love.
Here and above,
Now are here for you,
To forever guide you down your path.
Now and forever,
You are loved from above.
You are blessed with many here,
Whom you, they love.
Believe this,
For it is your truth.
Don't hold yourself aloof,
For they will miss your light.

Allowing the Flow

Search. Believe. Know.
Pull in the energy of light, love, and healing.
That was the triad we formed today.
As you speak of the flow,
Know also to visualize the triad.
Call all who need it to enter, ground and release.
You need not do the work.
You just need to visualize the connection.
Being aware and willing is the key,
To open the gate.
Many will come to enter.
Many will assist, just be present.
Know you have a connection far more than you know.
It is an orchestra of work we put together.
Time is coming for the connection to be reinforced.
To strengthen the bond,
As it becomes known on the spiritual plane.
Many seek a new way which they yet do not know.
People's spirit will enter so they can assist the soul,
To heal and return to the vibration of love.
This they do as they enter your space.
That is a part of the journey for all souls now.
Be the light.
Be the power as you work.
Let no one make you wavier.
You are never alone.

Angel's Wrap

Many friends you have had,
Who loved you.
Many who hold,
Your greatest good in their mind.
You give out and now need to receive.
Bless this as you allow these gifts to be yours now.
Receive from above and below.
Heaven and earth will help keep the flow.
Receive from all four directions.
Receive from humans,
As this will allow their light to grow.
Take the love as your food,
As it nourishes your needs.
Allow the love,
And know it, you so truly deserve.
This love is here to serve your health,
Your soul, your spirit and your life.
Let go of all past loves or lack of love,
For now, you have the greatest love.
From Above, Below and Within your realm
As it continually flows into and around you.
When you have a need,
Just pull an imaginary string.

It'll bring an abundance of love and good things,
As it is here forever to stay,
To calm, to nourish, to replenish, to fill.
It never empties, it's always full.
You have a precious path,
To walk on the earth.
Many places to see,
Many places to go.
You have riches
Far beyond what you know.
Rebirth. Relive and Be Alive.
Sparkle with this glow.
We are always there,
Never far away.
Just call us,
To feel our peace.
Believe. Believe. Believe.
Rise above what you use to know,
For it's broken away,
From your newly developed soul.
My Love, my faith.
My support will never die or leave you.
This now starts a part of life anew.

Daily Guidance

Life is sometimes a challenge.
Allow yourself to flow in the direction which feels the best.
Be aware of how you feel as you go through your day.
Ask your spirit to let you know what is yours,
Or what you might have picked up during the day.
Uneasy or negative emotions are being thrown out all the time,
As you walk your journey you sometimes become the sponge.
Now intend to be the sieve through which stuck emotions may pass.
Your Spirit, Angels, and Guides are waiting.
They need to know you want to release them.
So every day, ask for help to set them free.
See them taken by the wind for the universe to recycle.
It is our hope and our dream to assist you in making a happier life.
Know we watch you from afar, always ready to serve.

Fear

In fear, I've lived,
In darkness and pain.
In fear, I never knew any gains.
In fear, my world was destroyed.
In fear I lived and continued,
To breed life the same way.
Pierced from an angel above.
I came to live only in love.
Today it's a new way.
A new way not only for today,
Only forever and a day.
Look above and see the light,
Seen only by keen eyesight.
It's the way you go today,
Running and jumping,
As you play today.
Free at last from the past.
Living in love only love.

Anger

A feeling I sometimes have.
A place to hide
And used to push you away.
Sometimes it erupts
Or it is in control.
Sometimes it can come up
And I can work through it.
It is hard and takes perseverance,
But worth the fight if you can go the distance.
Some people don't want to fight,
The anger hides in their heart.
It is easier to hide,
And to pretend we don't know, it's there.
A dangerous, destructive emotion.
It slowly eats away at your insides.
Eventually, it will destroy you
And others in your life.
A sad state of affairs,
When we allow it to be in our life.
Beware! Do all you can!
Don't allow this, to eat away at your life.
Look deep into all motives and habits.
It's worth the fight and as it comes into the light,
Your life improves beyond measure.
Your body improves because it has more energy,
As it no longer has to fight just to hold on.
So, let go and live well
For yourself and others.

Healing

We come and go, here and there.
Looking and searching,
And it all leads to nowhere.
It is not without, it's within,
That we can go to heal and live again.
A journey, sometimes long, because we make it so.
Sometimes we can't see or let go, so we can begin to grow.
Our hurts, our pains do not need to be relived again.
It only needs to be looked at and see how it gave us our pain.
Let it go. Let it be.
For it only hurts you.
Power it gives when you don't let yourself live.
Those who hurt you know not your pain,
But some would feel glad,
If they knew you relived the pain again.
This I refuse to give.
So I will decide it's my life to live.
I will live free of old hurts,
Because this is mine not their life to live.
It is a choice and sometimes a rocky road,
But a wonderful journey, that's your real life to live.
Replace the unknown you with the pieces you find
As you walk through the old strife.
The pieces you find, make up the new joy.
It is different and has stronger glue.
Life falls apart less because you are new,
Not battered and knocked about,
By emotions as they come unglued.

You now become who you really are,
Not what were your scars.
It is like night being filled by the sun.
Now new and complete you look for new things.
Old memories and people, past hurts and places,
Need never happen again.
You'll change as you go.
You'll fill the void.
You are lifted inside as you pulled the pain out.
It's now your choice of what fills the void.
Happier, calmer and more approachable you become.
For people to know you and where you come from,
Not the old you which to them was full of pain and unapproachable.
Walk each step knowing others walk beside you,
For they also journey inside.
Follow those you see have gone ahead.
They are changed sometimes still changing,
As their life becomes more fulfilled and happier too.

Hidden Within

Where is the love that has no joy?
Where is the seed that doesn't get sown?
Where is the field that does not get tilled?
It's that piece inside that has not been found.
It's your core self, the part you don't know.
It is so anxious because it wants to grow.
It's God's gift to yourself and this great world.
It's a blessing for you to give to this world,
As there are none who have your greatness.
Know, Develop yourself,
To find your blessings.
Don't deny us you as we are waiting
And anxious to see the whole self,
As a glimmer, we can already see.
So go inside and find that place
And bring it out for you and me.
I wait for I see the glory of that self you are.

Know This World As One

Know this is one world.
Know that it is time to unite,
As *ONE*.
It is from the space of one,
In heart, mind, body, and soul,
That you heal, and that the world heals.
Nations lead people,
And it is time,
For people to lead nations.
This is the way of oneness.
To heal it must be from the heart.
You must be first
As you are a light which shines.
Give awareness and gentleness to yourself first.
Bathe in the awareness of being important and worthy.
Allow this to expand as you are nurtured.
Focus within and take a golden strand,
From your heart.
Pray as you weave it around the world,
As you play with this see it go to every country.
See it anchor awareness and peace.
See it touch everyone.
Know you have the power.
The power of *ONE*.

As you create awareness and peace
You support everyone.
Encourage all to be aware.
Encourage all to play with the light.
Encourage them to weave this in their own way.
See Know. Feel. Be.
Be the awareness of the power you hold,
Inside your *ONE* body,
This *ONE* can change and lead.
Be filled with the courage to go forth and be the *ONE*.
Be aware. Be Free.
Be the *ONE* who heals and leads.
Be that *ONE* in the sea of humanity.

The Chiropractor

You are here to serve us
And make our bodies well and mobile.
Gentle, patient, kind, aware and knowing.
You do the work.
You create a new space in us.
You give us freedom from our restrictions.
All of you create a sacred space and time.
You work together as you all move about the office.
The energy flows, bringing in the energy of peace.
Know you are guided in your work.
Allow the energy of light and love to flow through your hands.
This will increase the effectiveness of your work.
It flows like fingers of light through your hands.
Caring about and caring for others is a blessing.
You create wellness within the body,
That flows to the mind and then the spirit.
The spirit can then assist with more ease,
Because restrictions and blocks are lessened.
Remember you are the gift that makes the body better.
It is for this, their spirit thanks you,
As it helps free their souls.
Blessings to you all.

Grandchildren

To Nicole and Justin
And all the grandchildren we love.
A gift, a blessing I cherish each day.
My pride, my joy
And one of life's great pleasures.
This is for all children.
Our budding,
Lawyers,
Doctors,
Entertainers,
Waiters.
Waitresses.
Plumbers.
Writers.
Floor cleaners.
Dishwashers.
Mediators.
Politician,
Too many to name.
Know you are loved as you are,
No greatness needed

As She Walks

As she walks through the day
On this beautiful green earth.
She rushes and runs,
To do all her work.
She never says No,
Just keeps putting out.
It's time to *STOP*
And say No, No, No.
Time to replenish.
Time to find the inner core.
Time to breathe.
Time to explore.
Walk-in all your Beauty,
Each step you take for this is part,
Of the gifts to us you make.
Life is your garden
As well as your home.
Breathe in the Beauty,
As you do, you find so much more.
Time for yourself,
To replenish your space.
Time to give,
To your family and your faith.

Your beauty, your spirit,
Your grace is forever renewed,
At the beginning of each day.
Never allow yourself,
To be drained as this slows,
Your life's beautiful train.
Stand in your own place
And do not waver.
Your gifts and your life,
Are too Precious to waste.
Use love as a path in life,
For it will delete strife.
The joy, the happiness, and the love,
Are all the gifts we need to give.
Walk life's road using these each day.
So you may walk in light on your own pathway.

I Am Me

I am me.
I am a sad me at times.
I feel like I've walked a long road.
I know not where I've been at times or how I got there.
I just walked to where I was led.
I saw no light within me.
I felt old.
We ask you now to like you.
Look for the good in you
That's what we see.
Your past is past.
Allow us to now help you to create a NEW you.
To do this you must look within.
Find what we see.
You are not alone.
We walk with you on this journey.
I am starting to see me now.

Leaving

It is sad at times as we don't let go.
It is yearning for that which we don't have.
We delay so we don't have to go,
Back to the reality of our everyday life.
We don't think about what,
We have gained in our life and on this trip.
We can remember in our minds,
The views. such beauty.
As I leave, I will always remember the beauty
And the joy it gave me.
This I will carry with me.
I thank the creator for all the beauty
And the chance to travel here.

Life's Lessons

We are on a journey which we do not know.
A journey in trust of our guidance.
It comes from without and within where it begins.
Journey inside so you may see,
As we learn lessons that sometimes turn us inside out.
Know you are safe and protected too,
Always keep looking for the lesson for me and you.
Travel this road in life, sometimes lonely, sometimes free,
But always worth doing for you and me.
Life gives you lessons that you might see,
That they point to the path on which you need to be.
Life gives you freedom and wisdom.
These are also lessons for you to look at too.
Go forth on this journey with hope and joy,
For if you follow it, you'll be overjoyed.

My Angel

She is love which I receive even when I disbelieve.
She is joy pushing me there over and beyond all my fear.
She is persistent even as I am resistant.
Because I feel insane filled with thoughts of sadness, fear, and pain.
She's Prodding and pushing me through negative thoughts and sad feelings.
She lifts my feet when I'm too angry, sad or blue.
She had a hard job at times for I was resistant and had no hope.
I thought I was drowning and had no one to care or throw me a rope.
Little did I know her power and grace,
As she walked with me even when I fell on my face.
These lessons allowed me to learn so I might value peace, love, and joy,
Leading me just around the bend to see the world
And my life as it was meant to be.
She walked with me when I fell, she watched me cry and rage.
She accepted these and watched me let go.
She loved me through each sad page.
This was her greatest gift to me,
I got through and beyond that time in life.
I've learned, that I brought that grief into my life,
Through some of my choices.
I walked through and let go,
To test different thinking and learn new feelings.
She waited there in Joy and Love,
Which I still continue to receive from above.

Thank You

Angel Star.

New Dawns

As you enter into a new dawn,
Release the old which no longer serves you.
Humanity and the Earth recognize you are the spark,
The seed, the glow, the fire of the presence here.
This is part of a new earth for all of humanity.
As you find and live this, you change
And this will change the world.
It is your gift.
Be Love.
Be the Light

Blessings

My Space

A safe comfortable space.
Important, a part of me.
A place to be happy, sad, joyous and free.
Free to be me.
The positive and the shadow,
The fears and feelings.
The place of non-judgment,
Only acceptance.
The place I learn who I am
And who I am becoming.
A cocoon of beauty and light,
Nurturing my soul.
A sometimes-private place
For my essence and me,
My beauty and grace.
A place to grow and learn and discern,
All the universe wants me to know.
Life's lessons I needed to know,
So I could grow.

Divine Love

Be present.
Feel the air.
Know the Divine is present.
Know you deserve the Divine Presence.
Life is changing.
Allow the Divine to come to you.
It is time.
Accept it now.
You are a great source of *LIGHT.*
Allow it to be with you.
Know it is the truth.
Be free and allow Divine Love to fill you.
Allow.
Know it is time.
Be open to what you don't see.
Love always flows freely.

February
The Divine Energy is bubbling into the mist which
becomes your mantle of all you need.
Accept this as our gift to you as you step away and be our vehicle
for the Divine to enter into your world. The time is here
and this energy is needed throughout your world.
Be the maker of the mist which you then allow
to be a gift you give to the world.
To do this simply think of stepping back and allowing your
soul to channel the energy out into the world.
You are just the receiver which assists you
And that is all you need to do.
Blessings

Life Is a Precious Gift

Life is a precious gift
That we live each day.
Awaken yourself.
Stop being on autopilot.
Life is what it is.
When we are happy in ourselves as we are
Nothing needs to change for fulfillment.
As we allow ourselves,
To be and feel in the present moment.
We *simply connect* to the Divine Source.
We are the Light.
We are the Love the universe deserves.
Allow yourself to give the gift of Light and Love from the Source,
To the world and all, it holds in it.
KNOW
ALLOW
BE
ACCEPT
FEEL
Be the mist (of Niagara Falls)
You can allow that power to flow beyond you.
It is done.
As it is done you give the gift of the Universe to the entire world.

March 17, 2016

Inside

I have seen the Journey
From here to there.
It has its lessons
For it is fired anew.
The place of life.
The place of peace.
The place of self within the inner space.
Go forth to that space inside.
Here is the knowledge that resides within.
You are to start your journey.
You are your light.
You are the God that resides within.
You are the seed.
It is time to grow.

Light A Candle to Peace

Light a candle to Peace in this world that you
And all others may live in peace.
Light a candle to peace in your heart,
That you may forgive all who have hurt you.
Light a candle to peace
And ask that a loving nature guide your life.
Light a candle to peace
And may it be inside yourself each day of your life.
Light a candle to peace with yourself.
Light a candle to peace that we may live
Our lives in freedom.
Peace be with you and me.

Thank You

Live Life to the Fullest

Live life to the fullest.
It's a precious gift,
For you Gods Child.
A joy, a wonder, a dream.
Find your own peace inside,
To know yourself.
May you find your joy and dreams,
For they are greater than they seem.
Your life is a gift to all of us,
So precious to behold.
May you know this and more as you grow.
You hold inside all these dreams.
Let them out for they need to be seen.
Life will flow in a wandering way
As you search for all you need.

Who am I?

Who am I today?
A woman of beauty,
Who knows spiritual things
And who wants to do those spiritual things.
One loved by many,
Liked by many more.
Looking for my path
To live in love, abundance, and joy.
Mine eyes, my heart,
My spirit, my soul.
These are now open to all I know,
To blend in life with love and joy.
I will walk this path
With ease and grace.
Because I know
It is my place.
Loved, supported
Held and taken care of.
From some on earth
And many above.
I heal, with their help,
The old wounds and past karma.
I am leaving no more room,
For illness or old drama.
Life will be my pleasure
Without illness or censure.
Changes to make
With these shifted beliefs.
Joy and happiness
Are mine to keep.
Now so worthy and valued
By others and myself anew.
I go forward with confidence and grace,
To take my new place in this human race.
Moving upward and forward
In abundance, with self-worth, joy, and grace.

Our Song

Through wandering ways,
We get where we belong.
Some of the times we are full of sorrow,
But then again, we are full of song.
Some of our songs we sing inside,
Others we sing to others on the outside.
Our songs are the best of ourselves,
Those things we don't always see,
But sometimes we get help from our human elves.
They help us know the soul of us,
That we may show the world our light.
That is our path.
It is our purpose to be this light.
For ourselves, others and so that all souls may see the light,
To show them that spot inside that God and others know.

The Angels Come In

As we walk through life, through heartache and pain,
They help us keep moving forward through the pain.
Sometimes feeling lost and alone,
Sad and in pain,
We often believe there will never be hope again.
Know that you are never alone
As you walk life's long road.
You are helped to go step by step
To find the end of the pain.
This road goes on past sadness and pain.
It's when we do our part that we get to joy
And begin to live again.
The road goes on as changes come around each bend.
It's called life and watched with love
From your Angels in heaven above.

The Gift of Life

We come to life.
We perceive only what we know.
This is a limiting life.
So we ask our conscious self to know,
Who we really are.
There are many things,
We feel we can't achieve.
That is not the truth,
As our subconscious is unlimited.
Be willing to know,
All that you don't know.
Allow yourself to remember,
As it guides your life's flow.

Their Life

Her, the center of His life.
He, the star of her life.
Both encompassed by love
And faith in each other,
That abounds and is so great.
Stars and the universe shine
On these precious people.
They grace our earth
And add blessings to it too.
So, blessed are they.

Touching a Soul

You come into a life
And change it for the better.
Your words, your care, your compassion,
your spice, all add up to the love,
You give to prolong life.
It's a gift few give
As they go through each day,
Giving to others,
Touching someone in special ways,
Is a wondrous thing these days.
Each soul is better for your care.
It's life's journey that you share.
No riches, no rewards
On this earth's plane.
Just remember a soul's journey
Was made better again.
Go forth each day
As you always do,
Knowing your gift.
It is the greatest thing.
Your gift of caring
Makes a difference
To each soul.
Death's passing may come,
But life's journey is not done.

It extends beyond into all space,
To live within God's grace.
The souls are aware
Of how much you care.
This lightens their journeys
Of which you are unaware.
Blessings to you,
That may never end,
As you help right to the end.
Your grace, your kindness, your loving care
Make each person's life rich with what you share.
Lighter loads, welcoming light
On each journey to the light.

Throughout our life, we touch people every day. This is a gift of
enlightenment as you care about others. As we are around people toward
the end of their life the simple act of caring makes their last journey
easier. This caring is love which helps them on the journey,
it envelopes them like a blanket.

Trust

Let go of all past loves or lack of love,
And know you have the greatest love.
Coming from above, below and within your realm,
As it continually flows into and around you.
When you a have a need just pull a string.
It'll bring forth an abundance of love and good things.
These are here to stay to calm, to nourish.
To replenish, to fill.
It never empties for you,
As you are too good.
You have a precious path,
To walk on the earth.
Many people to see,
Many places to go.
You have riches,
Far beyond what you know.
Rebirth, relive and be alive.
Sparkle with the glow.
We are always there,
Never far away.
Just call us
To feel our peace.
Believe, believe, believe.
Rise above what you needed to know,
For it has broken away,
From your newly developed soul.
My love, my faith,
My support,
Will never leave you.

This now starts a part of a new Angel Wrap which is when they wrap their energy around us so that we can be supported as we go through life. This will happen at various times but also when we are in crisis or going through changes. They gave me this message for everyone as I was going through a serious health situation.

Written in the hospital 10/29/2000

Two Sides of Life

Ripples gently flowing.
Sun glistening on the blue-black water.
Hills and mountains.
Light and dark evergreens.
Limbs flowing north.
A touch of red and yellow mixed in.
Look at the other side.
Steel-blue water
With glistening stars.
Gentle hills and mountains behind.
Gentle swells with glistening peaks.
Wonderful trees and cottages to.
These are the scenes as we go down the road.
Both with beauty reminding us,
There are always two sides to choose from.
We can go straight and just look ahead,
Or we can be open to the different pictures
And choices on both sides.

What Will Happen to Me?

Cold, alone,
Sad and angry.
Hiding, hiding,
From me and thee.
Stay away.
I don't want you to know me.
I'm afraid and don't want to see,
Who I am or who I will be?
Excuses are cold and empty,
Saying, oh well, I don't want to stop.
I say the words,
I think they want to hear.
When, Oh when
Will I change?
When, Oh when
Will I refrain from self-destruction?
It is an internal soul choice,
That I must make,
For there's much I can be.
It scares me for it means it's my responsibility.
This journey we can take,
But it's not one we can fake.
Hard, difficult and sometimes lonely.

But it'll be an honest journey we can make.
Reach out, reach inside,
For that is where you hide.
Reach inside and find, there you are,
The beautiful person you hide inside.
Choices are not always easy.
Choices are about your life.
Choices can make or break you,
And this is the most important one for you.
It is about happiness.
It is about being free of anger, fear, and hate.
It is about life and death.

Grow through it all.
Be the real and true YOU.

Wish Upon a Star

When you wish upon a star,
It comes to you wherever you are.
It sometimes has trials or tribulations.
It twists and it turns upon its way,
As it enters into your life today.
It brings what you need
To help you grow beyond a small seed.
The seed grows
And a beauty it becomes.
Look for the star seeds
In your life.
They are the successes, the good,
The joy, the fun.
Look up and call it to you.
Look for it in your life.
Look for changes in yourself.
Look for changes in the world.
These are the Star's seed.
This is your wish coming.
This is you,
Becoming all you are meant to be.

Within This World of Chaos

I find Angels.
Unknown to them as they do not see,
It is them.
They are cheerful, patient,
As they live life,
They enhance others.
Gentle souls living life.
Unknowing they are a gift to others.
Calm and peaceful,
Wise giving souls.
Those touched by them
Are blessed indeed, as they are helped,
In their time of need.
As they move, they leave behind a glow.
This is healing and peace created by them,
Without conscious thought.
Guided through all they do.
It is a journey of giving life.
Many are blessed by their gifts.
And we give great thanks from all who received.

You are Here Today

You are here today
To feed your soul.
Know it is time for you to expand.
Be the blessing that you are.
Do not feed worry, anger or doubt.
You do not see the real you.
You only see your false face.
So be brave and look within.
It is not a hard task,
But be aware it is *necessary.*
Be the light and allow it to expand.
You are a gift.
You are the light.
Find your light and live it.
That will lead the way,
With the things you teach today,
Into the new age.
A Blessing,
A gift to all on your journey
As your walk enhances all life.

We Are Always here

We are always here.
We never leave you.
One of us may leave for a short time,
But we always come back.
We have waited for the day you find you.
You are a Blessing, which you cannot deny,
As we see you as you truly are,
And not as you see yourself.
Be aware of all aspects of yourself.
Each emotion is a part of you.
Choose the ones you'll be,
Not the ones which run on autopilot.
The time is now.
Change has started.
Be alive.
Be Free.
Be all you can be.
Blessings from us.
I have always held you in my arms.
You choose to not know this.
Stop. Feel my presence.
Be willing to receive help.

My Land Traveler

To you, we give our Precious Gift.
To look at our deeds.
To find our precious seeds,
For that is our need.
A precious gift you have
And for this we are glad.
Spirits of Nature, Earth,
Wind, and Sky
For this, we cry.
We watch as you grow
And you may call on us as you know.
A puzzle we can unscramble,
As you walk among us in the brambles.
Journey with us to the place
As we help with the sacred space.
A journey you do not yet know
Will take you from here to the new inner space.
There you will find the place to recline.
To live, to grow,
To learn more about all you know.
The spirits come in to help bring it about
Bring it in, bring it out
Bring it out, bring it in.
Topsy, turvy we will spin,
To bring the earth in balance again.

Gentle then we fall
To the ground among us all.
This is the gift we give
As we learn how to live.
Important you will be
As you walk the Earth with me.
A trail you leave behind,
In a pattern to which you're blind.
The explanation you will someday know
But it's a journey on which you must go.
A trail you leave among us now,
That will lead the way,
With the things you teach today,
Into the new age.
A Blessing,
A gift to all on your journey
As your walk enhances all life.

Peace Within

I intend that I will allow all that I need to process through me.
You are the Peace of the Universe.
You are the essence of this peace.
You are the Creator of all that is.
You are the Creator of life.
You are the whole.
You are the Soul.
You are the Being of the Blessed Peace.
You are the strength.
You are the Gift.
You are the Grace.
You are beyond what you know.
Be the Blessing.
Be the Gift.
Be Love.
Be Forgiveness.
Be the Peace.

I Am

Thoughts.

I am love. I deserve love.
I am free of doubt and limitation.
I honor who I am,
As I learn more about me,
I accept all parts of me.
I am a strong, beautiful and courageous person.
I know I will find guidance in my life.

Message sent by spiritual guides.

You are a person of great value,
Great love and compassion.
You deserve all life has to offer.
Know we will guide you.
Know you will come out of this
And create an unknown part of yourself,
Which will love all life.
Know this is a lesson.
Know you're never alone.
Life has many path's open for you.
This is who we all are when we can accept ourselves.

This Is You

Caring, giving with love and compassion,
Knowing this is the way we should all be living.
Beautiful, kind and joyous too,
Is the loving nature that shows through you.
Solid and trustworthy, a friend so true.
It's the nurturer we find in you.
Oh, blessed one be the nurturer to yourself first.
This is the most powerful way to replenish and to be strong.
This will make the journey easier if we are not drained.
Let sadness, anger and any negative emotion flow out of you.
It takes away that which holds you down.
A loving nature is hidden beneath that old stuff.
This old negative stuff no longer serves you.
We ask, "Why do you hold on to it?"
It is time to let go and allow your life to change for the better.

A Joy We Once Met

Kind, gentle and loving to all she met.
Full of fun and always kidding about the trouble,
You were in sometimes with a little help from her.
Joking and laughing were always around.
She loved her kids,
Always searching for the missing key,
To unlock the potential inside.
She never stopped until their potential we could see.
Many kids developed and grew,
Because of her dedication and persistence of a teacher who knew,
The unlimited potential of all to grow.
She loved and took great joy
In her family who through her we got to know.
Special they are and very blessed,
To have a wife and mother who celebrated their walk-in life.
A joy to work with.
A joy to know.
A joy to watch her help others grow.
A joy to have learned from our friend.
On her journey, she has done many things,
Helped many and was their friend.
This part of her journey has come to an end.
It is sad to lose our friend.
It has been a gift to have met her
And walked a part of her journey with her.

May the angels care for our friend Helen Addona
who was a precious gift.

Grandparents

A gift so precious you see
For the blessings we bring,
To our special children, you see.
Our humor, our values, our faith, our love
Are as precious as his love from above.
We support, encourage and care for those we love,
Knowing they are a gift from above.
Our guidance, our stories and our belief in them
As they do the tiniest task,
Is a joy for our world to see.
No pushing or shoving to get there first.
They share with each other that they may be joyful and free.
They are an example we'd like all in our country to be.
They make this world a better place for you and me.

How Do We Spend Our Life?

We enter into our lives in the arms of a family.
They care for us and try to nurture our needs.
As children we grow, we learn, we play,
And do all the things that children do.
School comes and we struggle with things.
Some we see no need to learn,
But that's not for us to discern.
Then come the teen years which are quite a struggle.
We date, we love hoping to live happily ever after.
Some things work.
Some things don't.
We do what we can and make the best of our lives.
We have children who we love and nurture,
Until it's their time to be on their own.
Then we look at our time left.
Feeling guilty for thinking of ourselves.
This is time to begin anew.
To do those things in our life we always wanted to do.
Look forward without guilt.
You've done all you could.
Time to enjoy.
Time to love.
Time to do all you wished you could have done.
The past is the PAST.
It is now a new day for you to enter and learn to play.
Keep not guilt.
Keep not pain,
As you enter a life you begin again.

Life is a Gift

Our life is a gift.
Do not waste it in any way.
Not just your body
But your mind and spirit are a part of the gift.
Go through your life
Being aware of all of you.
Where are you heading to?
What are you doing?
My mind!
Oh, what is it thinking?
What is it creating with these thoughts?
Oh dear!
That's where my spirit will go.
Life is so precious.
Do you hear this?
Do you really hear this?
Is that message being lost in space?
Be here! Be here now!
Make up your mind and be here now.
It is the driver of your life.
Control It. Guide It.
Look at what it thinks.
Look at what it's seeing,
Because from there you will become,
What it believes.
Look at the flow
That your mind has.
Look so you may see
The type of things you believe.
You are in charge!
You have the control!
So, see and you will know
That which restricts the flow.

Look for Yourself

Look into your world.
Look into your soul.
Look into your center,
For from here you will know.
Deep in your soul,
You will find the real you.
The one you really want to know.
So, search. Search inside of you.
Don't wait, go inside
To find out who you are.
Lookout from inside you.
Don't be scared. Don't stop and wait
Shed the "trappings
Of your old world.
Look at your life,
Your sadness and pain,
So you may recover and live again.
It's a blessing, a gift.
You have not known.
So, hurry inside and start to shift.
Throw out and off,
That which does not really fit.
Allow in that which feels good,
As that is where you find your special fit.
I watch, I wait,
For you to grow,
So, the real you, I may know.

You Are A Star

You are a star.
Which came from the sky,
That was within the Heavens above.
Created in beauty and love,
Without boundaries,
As the skies above.
Open and unlimited with the freedom to be,
The exceptional person
You were meant to be.
A journey,
A life with lessons to learn.
So, you may blossom
And discern.
Grow, Live, Learn
And become all you are meant to be.
Use love as a path in life,
For it will delete strife.
The joy, the happiness, the love
Are all the gifts we need to give.
Walk the road
Using these each day,
So, you may walk with joy
On your pathway.

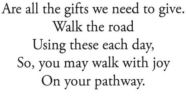

Life

Life goes around sometimes bringing a frown.
It is our choice to not be down.
Hard are these choices
Because our negative ego says, "*stay there.*"
It tries to keep us tied up in fear.
It doesn't want us to know
Where the mind goes is what will grow.
Bad or negative gets worse,
Positive or good thoughts will also slowly grow.
In hard times
Tell negative ego thoughts "*NO.*"
Change to positive thoughts
So, they too can grow.
You deserve so much,
This your negative ego doesn't know.
So, take your blessings of the positive,
Being sent to you by your Angels from above
And expand them in your life

You

You are a great person,
Who emits a loving vibration.
You need to learn to be in tune,
To the higher self of you.
This is how we can guide you,
When you allow us too.
Change is on its way.
Take time to find out about you.
You are more than you think.
We have always been near you.
Let the tears fall
And then move on.
Your new journey starts now.

You Are the Blessing

My life is different now and is filled with joy.
I have many friends who I see and enjoy.
I see the bright brilliant blue skies with the white puffy clouds.
I stand in the moonlight feeling its brilliant light.
There are many things to do and many places to go to.
I see many choices and hear all the caring voices.
So many thanks to you all,
You have touched me in many different ways.
You are the blessing for which in the beginning I could not pray

My Thoughts

Thoughts are things I draw to me,
Fleeting but permanent in the Universe.
I keep searching, mulling, reaching
And hoping to find the thought's source.
Clearer and clearer it now becomes,
As I see more how my thoughts guide me.
Thinking I was inadequate, unworthy
And undeserving, of all life 's good,
Not seeing its connection to me.
Subtle at times, hidden and hard to find,
These thoughts have raced around my mind.
I am now discovering and clearing these useless thoughts.
They knew not who I was and these are false beliefs I've been taught.
It is a part of life's necessary plan to improve my life and me.
Deserving, worthy and adequate I am.
As I think my own thoughts I live with more joy
And I come closer and closer to the inner God of me.

He, Who Can See

Strong, yet gentle,
Loving, yet firm.
Nonjudgmental,
To all willing to learn.
Softly he walks his path,
Leading us to our dreams,
We've found at last.
Supporting us
As we try to reach our goals.
Holding us,
Whenever we forget our goals.
Helping us to look inside,
To find our higher vision,
Where it resides.
He keeps us on track to obtain our vision.
Look in, look out, he says.
Here you'll pull out a vision,
A dream that never was.
It comes out
And now has a future.
Our mentor shows us how,
Our dream to nurture.
For him we give thanks
As he's opened another door.
One we didn't know and thought was just blank.
Blessings to this gentleman,
Who helps with dreams we can't ignore.

Little One

We are here.
We ask you to let go.
We Know you and all your secrets.
Do not hide.
Do not doubt.
You were created to be strong, wise
And a being of grace.
You are not alone.
You will never be alone.
Allow yourself to be free.
Love yourself beyond measure.
You deserve all good.
You deserve love, kindness and, peace.
Move forward in life loving you every day.
We will walk beside you.

The Vision

Where am I going?
Is this the story of my soul?
Will it nurture my soul?
If not, why do I go there?
I know the surface of me,
But do I see my inner glow?
It's that sacred place inside.
It is my soul.
The part I know that relates to the world
It's how I interact with what comes to me.
When I am in my sacred space I see it's glow.

The Searcher

She travels and searches
Through many lofty places.
Looking for more insights
From different places.
Searching for guidance and direction,
From lofts above.
She looks and searches
For a direction in which to move.
Go forth.
Do what you need,
To honor your space,
In this universe.
Blessings and love
Are sent from above
To honor and keep you,
Always in love.

Your Guides and Angels

You do not know us yet.
We know you.
We guide you through life.
Teen years are a challenge.
It is a time we all find our way through.
Trust yourself.
Ask us for guidance.
We will help you create,
What you want to do.
Be yourself.
Be confident.
Be true to yourself.
Know you are an awesome person.
Know you will succeed.
When you doubt call on us.
We are always here.

From your Guides and Angels.

This was written for a teenager but applies to us all.

A Divine Spirit

Divine Spirit.
Gentle Soul.
Questing, searching
For all, he can know.
Full of wisdom.
Full of love,
Sent to him,
From Heaven above.
Father sky,
Shine down on him.
Watching as he honors
The gifts he gives.
Blessed and ordained
His love heals,
As he joins with others,
To help them walk upon their healing path.

The Drains

A time in life
To nurture yourself.
A time you can do no more.
There is a reason for you to be here.
Let go, let knowledge in,
As you let go of fear.
The past is gone.
So, inside of you, don't let it hold on.
The tug and pull of old things,
Needs to be gone.
Put it in a bubble,
Keeping power and wisdom.
Place emotion inside the bubble
As you pull your energy in your body.
This is a key so, don't let go
Of the scared energy of your body.
That energy you allow to leak,
Drains and will never come back.
Pain, rage, and sadness
Are all negative emotions.
These are the drains
On your body's sacred energy.
It can leave so slow and subtle.
Moving from you,
As if running through a slow sieve.

Your strength, your energy cannot be replaced,
As it is part of your inner sacred space.
If it leaves, the good will also go,
Pulling you down, so don't let it go.
Pull back into your own power,
Keeping only that which benefits you.
Sadness, Pain, and Rage
Bring you down.
Love, joy, and hope
Are the way to not drown.
Keep yourself alive,
So we may know,
Your beautiful kind precious soul.
We all wait to see who you are,
Far below the old emotions.
Tear them away from your precious heart,
For that's the place to start.

The Light

The Light at the end of the tunnel.
It's always there.
Sometimes we do not see it,
Through our own fear.
Always keep looking,
When you feel lost and alone.
God's still with you as spirit knows.
It's sometimes a struggle to look through the dark,
For we only see fear and loneliness in our heart.
Tilt your head to see just beyond.
For the light at the end of the tunnel,
Is just beyond our closed mind.
Our sight falters in our fear,
And we need to remember,
God and Spirit are always near.
The light is God's love
And we are led there by Spirit.
It guides us always through all of life,
Which we do not see it's our home, our base,
The framework from which we come.
On our journey, we are led to what we need to become.
It's a journey, we need not fear,
As the light at the end of the tunnel will always be there.
It is the light which guides us out of the darkness,
So we may walk in joy and the excitement,
Of a life well lived.

Be in the Flow

Be in the flow of knowledge.
Trust your intuitive self,
As we guide you in this way.
Always be in the flow of energy.
Worry, fear, doubt,
And hesitation stops the flow of energy.
This stops what you request coming to you.
When you are aware of this pattern,
Ask for help to release fear,
And the need to suffer.
Time is now to change your habits.
We have created a unique time frame
For you to change.
Know we always guide you.
Be in gratitude as this helps the flow of good to keep coming.
You are never alone.

Message from the Angels

Hello
Be good to yourself.
Times are changing so be aware.
The energy has shifted and allows for new creations.
Be aware and ask all negative energies to release.
Push them all away.
See them in your mind leaving on a breath of wind,
Then feel the peace and find your core strength.
Build this strength, body, and soul, with love and light.
You are the creator of a new world.
It is your job, your purpose, your future.
We await you to create for us.
Have the courage to change your life.

The Gentle Way

Softly she Walks,
Upon her gentle path.
Searching for the lessons,
She is here to learn.
Healer of self.
She looks within,
To search for what to do,
For herself and others too.
Much learning.
Many openings,
Are now on the way.
Open to what fits for you today.
Walk forward,
As all will slowly come.
To build the skills,
Follow the energy,
The flow to each one.

Love

Many Times, Many Ways
People enter our lives.
Some for moments,
Others for the rest of our life.
They touch us
In ways we do not expect.
They teach us love,
They also teach us who we are.
Watch them,
Listen to them.
Love them
And watch yourself grow.
There are ups and downs.
There are highs and lows.
There is joy
But all is LOVE.
Open to others,
As yourself you allow them to know.
Open to them.
Honor you,
For the love you show.
Honors them as the love flows.
You give yourself the world,
As your love flows.

Live Life

Stop being on autopilot.
Life is what it is.
When we are happy in ourselves as we are,
Nothing needs to change for fulfillment.
As we allow ourselves,
To be and feel in the present moment,
We simply connect to the Divine Source.
We are *light.*
We are the love the universe deserves.
Allow yourself to give the *gift of light*
And *Love* from the *source,*
To the world and all, it holds in it.
Know
Allow
Be
Accept
Feel
You can allow the power of these to flow in and beyond you.
It is done.
As it is done, you give the gift of the universe to the entire world.
The Divine Energy of Love is bubbling into a mist,
Which becomes your mantle of all you need.
Accept this as our gift to you as you step away
And be our vehicle for the Divine to enter into your world.
This time is here now and this energy is needed,
Throughout your world.
Be the maker of the mist which you then allow
To be the gift to the world.
Step back and simply think of allowing your soul to send,
The energy into the world.
This takes our human doubts away as a more powerful source
Does the work.

The Centered Place

Centered in Peace she walks the Earth,
Knowing her connection to all things.
Giving this Peace to all as she walks past.
Always giving Love and Blessings.
Gentle, loving and kind,
She gives love and peace
To all those she finds,
Without them knowing what she leaves behind.
A part of nature,
A part of life.
A space of peace amid life's strife.
Gentle as a bird who enters your life.
Smoothly gliding, with gentle thoughts,
She touches us softly
As we walk, sometimes not aware
Of her touch.
A Giver, a Receiver
She balances both.
Always returning to nature,
To replenish herself.
She's blessed,
As we share her space
And say thanks for this gentle breeze.
We are calmer and more centered
Because she has entered,
And blessed are you and me.

Setting ourselves Free

We come and go, here and there,
Looking and searching out there which all leads nowhere.
It's not without, it's within,
That we find the courage to heal and live again.
A journey sometimes long, because we make it so.
Sometimes we can't let go so we can begin to grow.
Our old hurts and pains do not need to be lived again.
Let it go, let it be for it's only you it hurts.
Power it will give when you don't let yourself live.
Power to those and that from which it came from.
Those who hurt you know not your pain but some would feel glad,
If they knew you lived again through the pain.
This I refuse to give.
I decide it's my life to live.
I will live free of all old hurts
Because this is mine not their life to live.
It' a choice and sometimes a rocky road, but a wonderful journey.
Find and leave old hurts behind you.
Do not allow them not to rule your life.
Replace it with the new pieces you find as you walk beyond the old strife.
The pieces you find as you make a the new you.
It's different and has stronger glue.
Life falls apart less because you are new, not rocked and knocked about,
By emotions as they come unglued.

You now become who you really are,
Not who you were with your old scars.
It's like the night being filled with the sun.
Now new and complete you, look for new things.
Old people, hurts and sad places need never happen again,
For you'll change as you go.
You'll fill the void you left inside as you pull out the pain.
It's now your choice of what fills the void.
Happier, calmer, more approachable you become,
For people now know who you really are.
Walk each step knowing others walk beside you for they also journey
inside.
Follow those you see have gone ahead, using them as guiding stars.
Their journey has become less hard and not filled with dread.
They are still changing, as their life becomes more filled and happier too.
Your strength, your energy cannot be replaced, as it is part of your inner
space.
So don't let it go,
Pull back into your own power, keeping only that which benefits you.
Sadness, pain, and rage pull you down, love, joy, and hope,
are the way to not drown.
Keep yourself alive so we may know,
Your beautiful kind precious soul.
We all wait to see who you are, far below the old emotions.
Tear them away from your precious heart for that's the place to start.

Can You Receive?

I send you a gift today.
It is a chance to create a new life.
It is so hard to do within your minds,
Because you have the *ego*.
Today choose to ask it to step aside.
Today choose to do something new.
It is a simple task,
That can happen within you.
What a concept!
We will even help.
Can you allow this and let go of control?
You have nothing to lose and if you try it might get better.

God/Creator, I am yours today
Assist me and let me be guided by you today.
I come to you and this world with love and peace in my heart.
Forward I shall go
I will look for your guidance
I know you will put in my path that which is for the greatest good.
I will look for the Blessing in whatever comes into my day.
I am at peace as I walk this journey of life.
I am renewed as I give myself and control to you.
My burdens become lighter.
My eyes see new possibilities.

You can change God to Creator, Higher Power
or whatever your highest guidance is.

Xander

A prize. A Joy.
A blessing in our life.
One who knows many things.
One who struggles,
But finds his way through.
He does not always know the way,
But he manages to find the way through his struggles.
Bright, special and creative too.
He is like Harry Potter's owl,
He knows many things.
Gentle, kind and caring.
He cares for others as he walks through life.
His job is to overcome his anger,
And to believe this he can do,
As I know he can.
The next job is to allow us to care for him,
No matter how he feels.

Look in all directions

Look in all directions.
See the beauty of our earth.
Walk the path and pay attention.
The view is there for just a moment.
It then changes for the next beautiful moment.
The sky, the trees with brilliant colors.
The moving trees and water.
God created this for you.
Clear your mind.
This beauty need not be hidden from you.
As you walk through your day,
Please stop to play,
As you marvel at nature today.
Open your eyes to see a broader view
For this will help you see the world anew

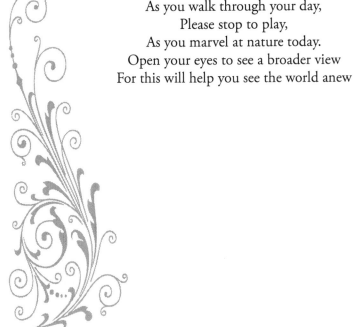

A Gathering

A gathering of people who are on a spiritual path,
That they may love and give their light out to the world.
It is a place in need of all good deeds.
Rich or poor it matters not.
A call comes to all.
Some will listen, some will not.
The call is soft on each ear,
So, come each to the gathering that's near.
Love, Light are our gift to you.
It'll lift you from the blues.
It'll send you deep in your soul.
It's a world waiting for you.

Made in the USA
Middletown, DE
10 January 2020

82387345R00080